Fancy dress for children's parties

Fancy dress
for children's parties

Anke Vogt

D-Books International-Hartlebury

productions
Craane/Timmies Ltd.
988 by D-Books International Ltd. Kiddermaster, UK.
he Old Rectory.

-2

uted by **Ruskin Book services Ltd.**

te

Kingdom

Contents

Foreword   6
General ideas   6
Tools   7
Materials   7
Banana   8
Directions for make-up   9
Patterns   10, 11
Orange   12
Directions for make-up   13
Patterns   14, 15
Kiwi   16
Directions for make-up   17
Patterns   18, 19
Lemon   20
Directions for make-up   21
Patterns   22, 23
Paprika   24
Directions for make-up   25
Patterns   26, 27

Apple   28
Directions for make-up   29
Patterns   30, 31
Strawberry   32
Directions for make-up   33
Patterns   34, 35
Grape   36
Directions for make-up   37
Patterns   38, 39
Pear   40
Directions for make-up   41
Patterns   42, 43
Cucumber   44
Directions for make-up   45
Patterns   46, 47
Raspberry   48
Directions for make-up   49
Patterns   50, 51

Foreword

The more we read, sing and play games with children or have a party, the richer their experience will be. They are excited by the idea of dressing up, and in fact it *is* exciting. Pretending to be someone else or even something else, fires their imagination.

This book contains advice for those who wish to make fancy dress parties with their children a real success. *Fancy dress for Children's Parties* contains 11 patterns for complete costumes based on fruit. The illustrations clearly show how you can transform your child into a banana, orange, pear or kiwi, to name but a few examples. The patterns are easy to use and the instructions are clear, ensuring that your creations cannot fail. The materials used for the costumes can be bought in any shop selling materials, or on the market. Old clothes or remnants of material can also prove to be useful.

In addition, the appropriate make-up is described in this book, as well as the costume itself. The make-up is described step by step with the help of examples in such a way that the costume and the make-up complement each other. The party is bound to be a success.

General guidelines

Patterns and sizes
The patterns in this book have been drawn to scale. Each square on the pattern is actually 4 cm x 4 cm. The pattern paper can be bought in craft shops and department stores.

The eleven costumes for children from 5 to 10 years old are marked small, medium and large. 'Small' refers to small children of 5 and 6 years old, 'medium' to 7 to 8 years old, and 'large' to bigger children aged 9 and 10. All the patterns for jump suits, shirts and trousers on the worksheets are marked 'S', 'M' and 'L'.

The 'fruit tops' and other 'covers' are shown in a single size, as these are worn over the costumes. These patterns can be enlarged or reduced as desired. It is a good idea for the child to try on the pattern before sewing up the costume, particularly to check the length of the sleeves and trouser legs. The fit is *not* the same as that for ordinary children's clothes. The patterns can be adapted by sewing the seams in a different place, or shortening or lengthening the sleeves or trousers legs.

An attempt has been made to give short and clear instructions, so that making these costumes is a simple matter. The jump suits,, tops and shirts are loose fitting. Awkward fastenings are replaced by elastic, Velcro, and hooks and eyes so that putting on and taking off the costume is not a problem — even for the smallest children. They will have complete freedom of movement in these party clothes.

Finishing off and fastening
The costumes are finished off with a small row of zig-zag stitching, a hem or with bias binding. The fasteners to be used include press-studs, hooks and eyes and Velcro. There is no need to use facing.

Stitching
The tops and capes are separate parts of the costume and they are reinforced by being stitched onto a layer of foam plastic. This foam plastic is about 1.5 cm thick and is available from virtually any shop selling materials or furnishing fabrics; it is better for this purpose than the usual fibre fill. Because of its rough surface the material can easily be pulled taut and does not move about when it is sewn.

There is no need for tacking the costumes; they only need to be pinned. Stitching may be difficult on a sewing machine, but this can be remedied in two ways:
(1) material is used on both sides of the foam plastic, though in this case you will need twice as much material;
(2) you stitch a strip of tissue paper or toilet paper onto the back of the foam plastic. This can easily be removed later.

Choice of materials
Light, stretchy materials such as cotton jersey, cotton towelling, thin cotton etc. are easy to use and generally not expensive. Use coloured and printed materials if you do not wish to dye the material. In this case it is also possible to use synthetic materials. In this book we have used both possibilities. If the materials are completely or partally dyed, it is better to use the former materials, either in white or in natural shades.

Dyeing
The costumes can be dyed in two ways:
(1) Cut the pattern pieces very large and dye the pieces before sewing them up. In this case you will not need such a large pan or tub as in the other method of dyeing. However, the disadvantage is that the foam plastic which is stitched on later stays a plain white.
(2) The pattern pieces are stitched onto the foam plastic and then dyed. In this case you will need a larger pan or tub than in the first method.
N.B. Jump suits, shirts etc. can be dyed in one go.
The best dye to use is made by Dylon and is available from chemists, supermarkets and department stores. You can choose between a cold water dye and a hot water dye. For the former you will need a large plastic or

enamel dyeing tub or washing-up bowl. For the other method of dyeing you need an enamel pan which can be used on the cooker. Follow the instructions on the packet carefully, mixing the dye and adding salt and/or soda. Dyeing materials in a variety of shades is a matter of practice, but can be great fun.

Example: the Pear
Ingredients:
One tin of yellow fabric dye,
one tin of green fabric dye,
one tin of orange fabric dye,
salt or soda,
white or undyed natural
material, foam plastic.

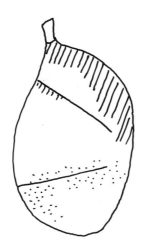

Procedure:
The two pattern pieces are stitched together without the stalk. Now follow the instrucions on the tin of dye to make the yellow dye. Both pattern pieces are dyed completely yellow and then thoroughly rinsed. Do not allow the material to dry after dyeing. Next prepare the orange dye. Submerge part of the pattern pieces in the orange dye, constantly moving them about while the dye is absorbed. This prevents a sharp line from appearing on the material. Again rinse thoroughly and do not allow to dry. The green dye is applied in the same way as the orange.
The wet pattern pieces can be lightly spin dried and then hung out to dry, though they should not be hung out in the sun or placed on a heater such as a radiator. When the pattern pieces are dry, they can be ironed on the front with a cool iron.

A useful tip: remember that the colour on wet material is much darker than when it has dried. It is therefore alright to 'exaggerate' a little when you are dyeing.

Another useful tip: you can use the same solution of dye to dye tights and other accessories, such as parts of the headdresses. In general you will not need to add any more dye than is indicated.

Tools

For doing the make-up of the appropriate 'fruit heads', you will need a mirror and a good source of light. Always work in front of the mirror so that you catch the light directly. It is useful to have a mirror on the table so that you can move about freely. A useful size for the mirror is 60 x 40 cm., though of course it is perfectly possible to use a mirror of a completely different size. An anglepose light is a very useful form of lighting.
For the make-up you will also need:
—   *sponges*; for applying the coloured make-up. The sponges are round and about 3 cm. thick, made of foam plastic with a rather greasy feel.
—   *a stippling sponge*: for coarse make-up;
—   *brushes*: in varying thicknesses;
—   *pencil sharpener*: for soft pencils;
—   *powder puff*;
—   *powder brush*: for removing excess powder;
—   *comb*;
—   *scissors*;
—   *chamois leather*: a piece of natural chamois leather, about 10 x 15 cm;
—   *case*: a fishing tackle case is very useful for storing all this equipment.

Materials

There are two sorts of make-up: greasepaint and water-based make-up. Greasepaint is a cream which covers less thoroughly, but is easier to blend in. Powder is needed to 'fix' the make-up. Water-based make-up is more resistant, but covers better and does not need to be powdered. You will need the natural basic shades of both these types. These are flesh tinted, lighter, darker, more red or more yellow, depending on the colour of the make-up. If you use water-based make-up, you will also need additional colours such as yellow, green, blue, purple etc. for applying the figures onto the basic make-up.
In addition, you will need:
—   pencils: soft, greasy pencils (dermatograph) so that lines can easily be smudged. These come in various colours;
—   powder: a neutral, light, transparant powder;
—   make-up remover, a type of vaseline for removing greasepaint. Water-based make-up can be more easily removed with soap and water;
—   soap: for washing the hands and sponges and, if necessary, for masking the eyebrows and the hair at the temples;
—   hairslides; slides and grips for holding the hair in place;
—   tissues for removing the make-up and cleaning the hands.

Banana

Material for the jump suit
Brown jersey 130 x 130 cm.

Material for the banana, hood and cape
White cotton jersey (washed), 150 x 120 cm.

In addition
Velcro
brown bias binding
hooks and eyes
elastic
one tin of yellow fabric dye
one tin of green fabric dye

◄1►
Cut out the jump suit from the brown material.
◄2►
Stitch the side and shoulder seams and the inside leg seam. Partly stitch the centre back seam.
◄3►
Hem the trouser legs, sleeves and neck. If necessary, thread elastic through. Fasten the centre back seam with hooks and eyes.
◄4►
From the foam plastic, cut the banana pattern 2 x.
◄5►
Cut the foam plastic banana shape generously 2 x from the white material.
◄6►
Pull the white material tautly over the foam plastic and pin it down.
◄7►
Stitch the material with a small zig-zag stitch on the front onto the edge of the foam plastic. It is easy to feel the edge of the foam plastic and it must be pressed flat while you are sewing. Stitch the seams to show the detail of the banana.
◄8►
Cut away the excess material.
◄9►
Cut the hood from the white material.
◄10►
Stitch the top seam and finish off the bottom with a hem.

◄11►
Cut the cap from the foam plastic and again from the white material. Sew up the hat like the hood.
◄12►
Make the foot coverings from the foam plastic and white material, like the hood and the cap.
◄13►
Prepare the yellow dye.
◄14►
Dye the cap, hood, hat and feet coverings according to the instructions. Rinse thoroughly, but do not allow to dry.
◄15►
Prepare the green dye. Submerge all parts partly in the green dye, one by one, moving them about while the dye is absorbed. Rinse thoroughly, dry and iron with a cool iron.
◄16►
The seams on the bananas can be marked more clearly using bias binding.
◄17►
Attach Velcro to the sides of the large sections of the banana.
◄18►
The shoulders are attached with tape.
◄19►
Sew the hat onto the hood.

Banana

1 A light yellow water-based make-up is applied with a sponge.

2 A few lines are drawn with dark brown make-up.

3 Another line is drawn across the middle of the face over the nose.

4 The lips are coloured with wine-red make-up.

Useful hints
Basic shade. Both greasepaint and water-based make-up are applied with a sponge. The sponge should be slightly damp. Take some make-up from the box with this sponge and apply to the face with a stroking movement from the middle of the face to the side, and from the top to the bottom.

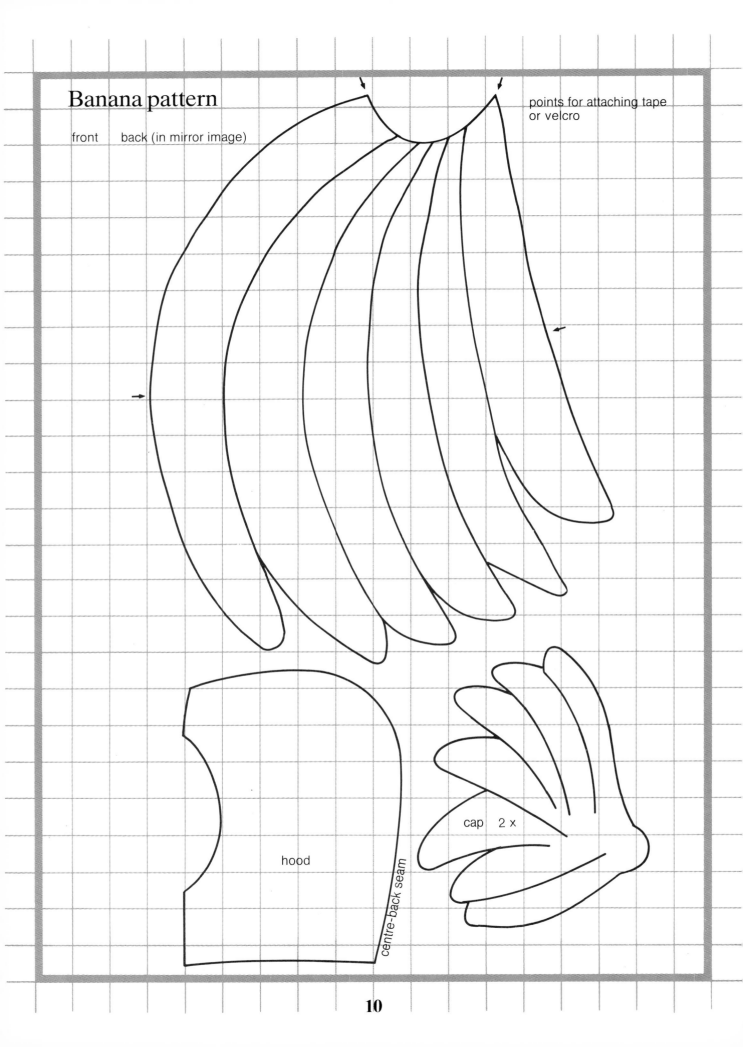

Banana pattern

front   back (in mirror image)

points for attaching tape
or velcro

hood

centre-back seam

cap   2 x

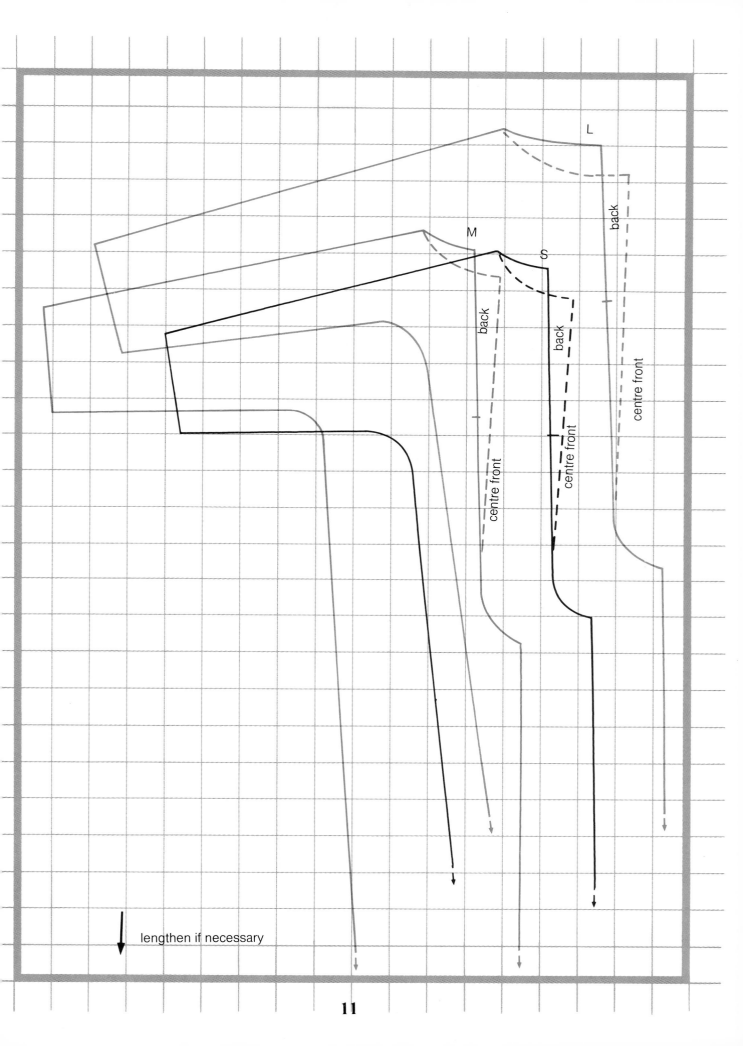

L

M

S

back

back

back

centre front

centre front

centre front

lengthen if necessary

11

Orange
Material for dress, top and hat

Orange jersey or lining material 200 x 120 cm.
1 jersey collar (ready-to-wear) white.
Foam plastic 60 x 120 cm.

In addition
hooks and eyes
orange bias binding

◄1►
Cut out the dress.
◄2►
Stitch the shoulder and side seams. Stitch the centre-back seam part of of the way.
◄3►
Hem the sleeves and bottom of the dress.
◄4►
Finish off the neck with the jersey collar. Fasten with hooks and eyes.
◄5►
Cut 2 x the sides of the top from the foam plastic. (If you wish to have a thicker segment of orange, you will need twice as much foam plastic.)
◄6►
Cut the same shapes 4 x from the material, leaving a border of approximately 3 cm. on all sides.
◄7►
Stitch these pieces of material together to form two cases, leaving some unstitched. Turn inside out.
◄8►
Place the foam plastic inside and sew up by hand.

◄9►
Stitch seams to form the pattern on the segments.
◄10►
Use bias binding or remnants of material to sew a ribbon on each end. Tie these together and drape the segments of orange around the neck like a sort of life jacket.
◄11►
Make the hat in the same way as the top.
◄12►
Stitch the segments together along the rounded edge.
◄13►
Finish off the bottom with bias binding, and then stitch along the top edge again.

Accessories
White tights
Appropriate shoes

For boys
Instead of making a dress it is possible to make a jump suit (see Apple, for example). Apart from this, the costume is the same.

Orange

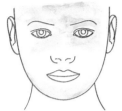   

1 A light pink water-based make-up merging into orange is applied with a sponge.

2 The segments are drawn onto the face with orange water-based make-up.

3 The top parts of the segments are filled in with light grey make-up.

4 White stripes are drawn with a thin brush. The lips are coloured bright red. Another line is drawn above the eyes with brown make-up.

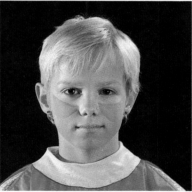

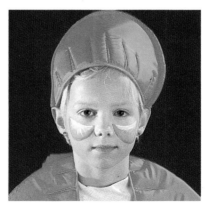

Useful hints
Applying the make-up. It is important to apply the make-up thinly and regularly, as thickly applied make-up shows up blotchy in bright light.

Orange pattern

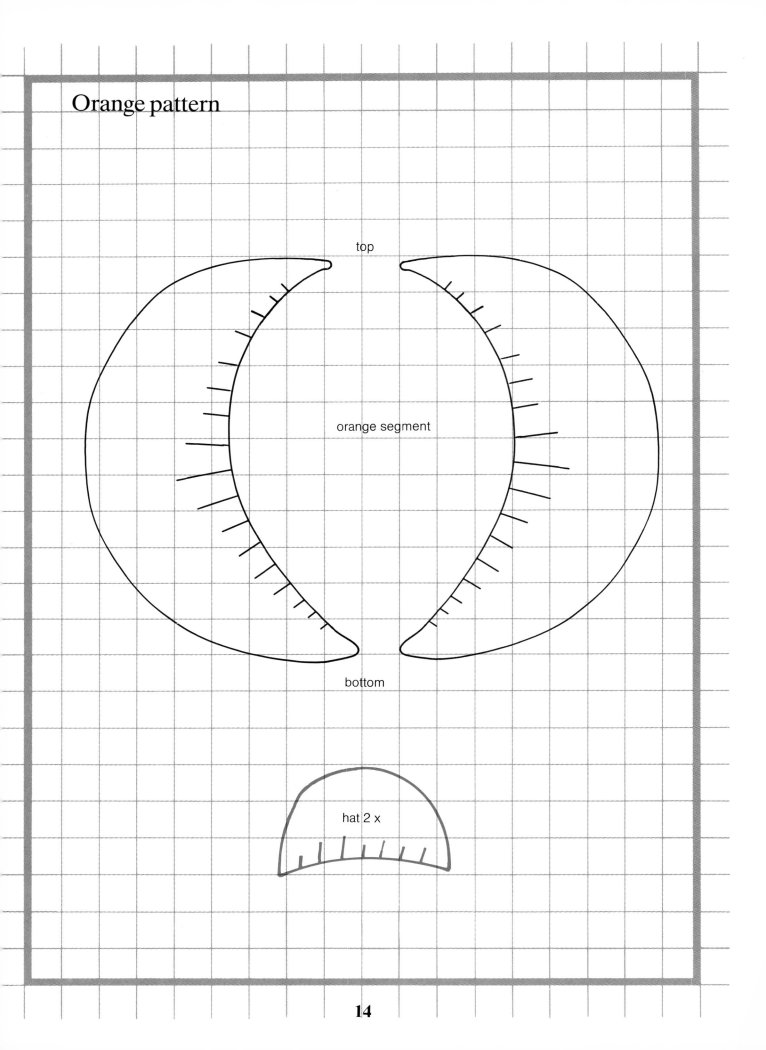

top

orange segment

bottom

hat 2 x

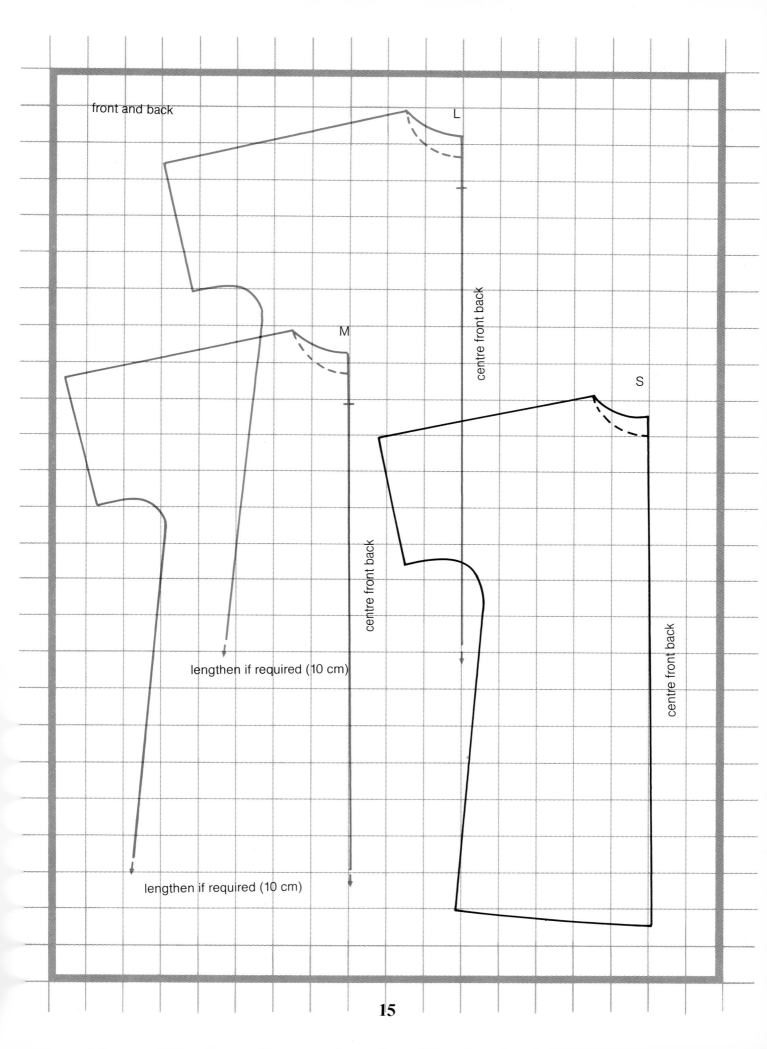

front and back

L

M

S

centre front back

centre front back

centre front back

centre front back

lengthen if required (10 cm)

lengthen if required (10 cm)

15

Kiwi

Material for jump suit
White cotton (washed) 200 x 120 cm.

Material for cap
Brown towelling 30 x 30 cm.

In addition
Foam plastic 40 x 60 cm.
Thin elastic
Hooks and eyes
One tin of green fabric dye
One black felt-tip pen for use on fabrics

◄1►
Cut out the jump suit.
◄2►
Stitch the whole front seam and the back seam up to the point indicated.
◄3►
Cut the kiwi fruit from the foam plastic.
◄4►
Place the kiwi on the cotton and cut out the shape leaving a generous border.
◄5►
Prepare the dye.
◄6►
Hold the kiwi material exactly in the middle and place almost entirely in the dye, leaving the centre outside. This remains white, and if the material is constantly moved there will be no sharp line. After the time indicated in the dyeing instructions, rinse the material and leave to dry.
◄7►
For both parts of the jump suit, dye only the ends of the sleeves and trousers legs in the same way. Then rinse these and leave to dry.
◄8►
Iron the dyed material with a cool iron.
◄9►
Place the kiwi material on the foam plastic and smooth it. Fold the border of the material back and pin it down.
◄10►
Place the whole thing on the front of the jump suit. The top of the kiwi should almost come up to the neck. Pin the kiwi and stitch along the edges onto the front of the jump suit.

◄11►
Stitch seams more or less as shown in the pattern.
◄12►
Mark in the tips with a felt-tip pen suitable for use on fabrics.
◄13►
Place the front and back of the jump suit right sides together.
◄14►
Stitch the shoulder seams, side seams and inside leg seams as far as indicated.
◄15►
Finish off seams, trouser legs and neck edge with a small hem.
◄16►
If required, put some elastic through the hem at the neck.
◄17►
Fasten centre back with hooks and eyes.
◄18►
Cut out the cap 3-4 x from the towelling material, depending on the size of the head.
◄19►
Stitch them together, hem round the edge or stitch bias binding along the edge. Pass elastic through to the required size.

Accessories
Green or brown tights
Plimsolls or similar shoes

N.B. The kiwi doll can be made with remnants of material and filled with fibre fill.

Kiwi

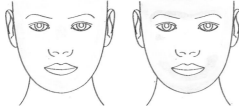  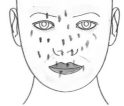

1 Green water-based make-up is evenly applied with a sponge as a base on the indicated part of the face.

2 A yellowish-beige greasepaint is applied evenly as a foundation, as shown in the illustration.

3 A narrow line of wine-red make-up is drawn round the eyes.

4 Dark make-up is used for the lips, and dark green lines are drawn on the face.

Useful hints
Use a thin brush (no. 6 or 8 eyeliner brush) to draw fine lines of dark green greasepaint over the whole face.

Kiwi pattern

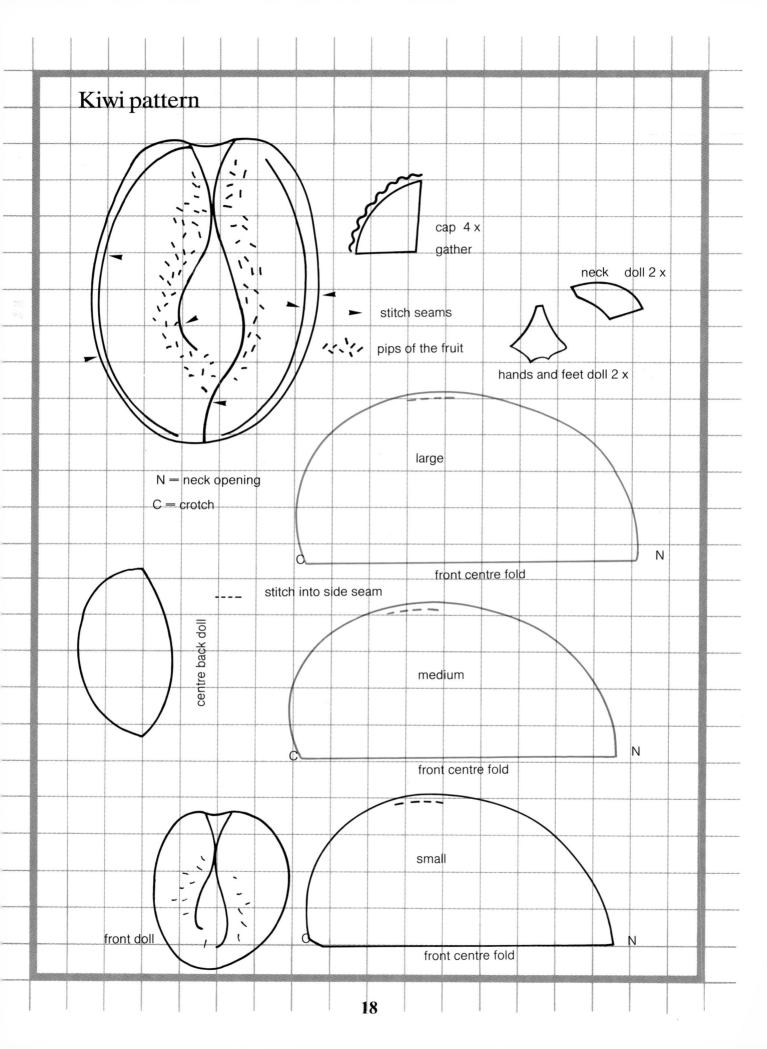

cap 4 x
gather

stitch seams

pips of the fruit

neck   doll 2 x

hands and feet doll 2 x

large

N = neck opening

C = crotch

C

N

front centre fold

centre back doll

stitch into side seam

medium

C

N

front centre fold

small

front doll

C

N

front centre fold

front and back

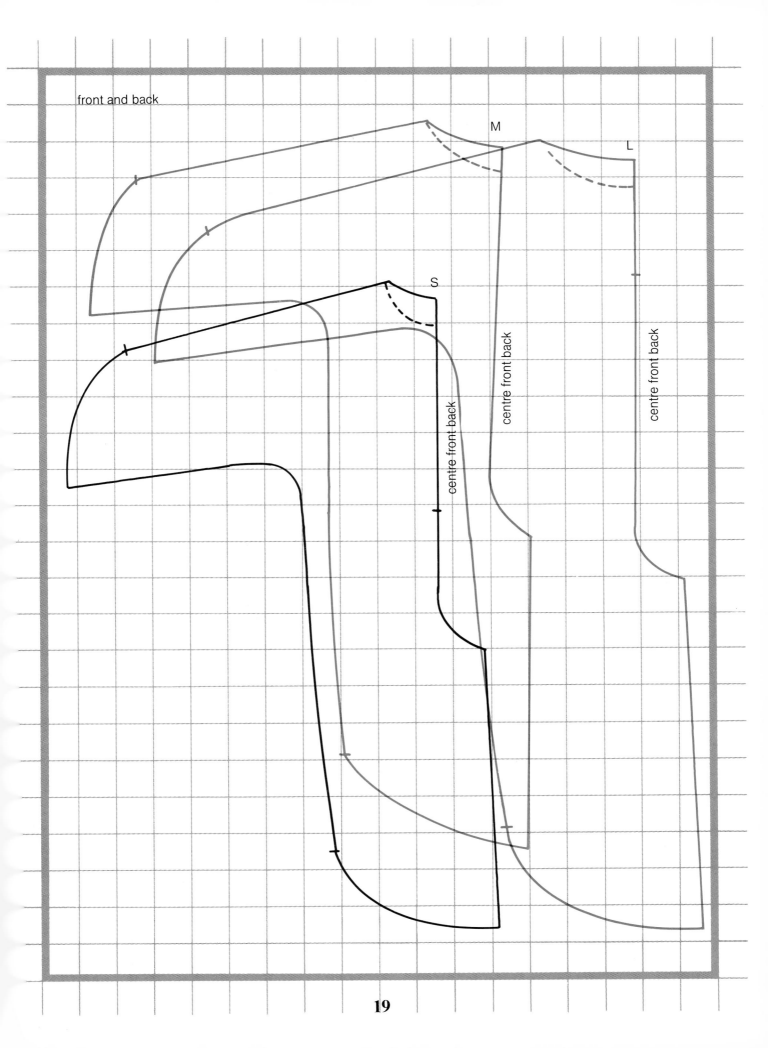

M

L

S

centre front back

centre front back

centre front back

19

Lemon

Material for the jump suit
White jersey (washed) 120 x 120 cm.
Foam plastic 50 x 120 cm.

Material for lemon
Yellow cotton or jersey 50 x 120 cm.

In addition
One tin of yellow fabric dye
One tin of green fabric dye
Elastic, wide elastic for gathering
Press-studs

◄1►
Cut the jump suit from the white material.
◄2►
Stitch shoulder, side and inside leg seams.
◄3►
Finish off neck, sleeves and trouser legs with a small hem and thread elastic through. (This can also be done after the material has been dyed.) Fasten with a press-stud.
◄4►
Prepare the yellow dye.
◄5►
Follow the instructions on the packet and dye the jump suit yellow. Rinse thoroughly but do not allow to dry.
◄6►
Prepare the green dye. Hold the jump suit at the waist and submerge the remaining ends in the green dye. Move the garment about until the dyeing process is complete. Rinse thoroughly and dry.
◄7►
Cut pieces AB 2 x from the foam plastic.
◄8►
Cut the same shape from the yellow material leaving a generous border.
◄9►
Stretch the material tautly over the foam plastic and pin.
◄10►
Stitch the material onto the foam plastic with a small zig-zag stitch exactly along the edge. It is easy to feel this edge and hold it down flat while you are sewing along the front.

◄11►
Cut part A (2 x) from the white material, leaving a generous border. Sew part A onto the yellow material by hand, and fold back the top edge.
◄12►
Stitch the seams to make the pattern in the white material.
◄13►
Stitch the side seams of both halves halfway down.
◄14►
Sew press-studs at the top.
◄15►
Gather the bottom with elastic.
N.B. The lemon should be quite full and therefore fit loosely. To make extra sure, you can sew a tape into the side seam of the jump suit, which can be tied to a tape on the lemon.
◄16►
Make a few segments of lemon and leaves, using remnants of material and foam plastic, and attach randomly over the costume

Accesories
A yellow shawl worn round the head, Eastern fashion.
Transparent yellow tights.

Lemon

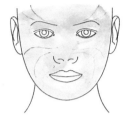 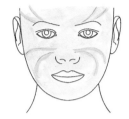 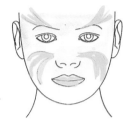 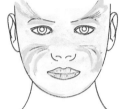

1 Apply a light-pink water-based make-up with a sponge.

2 Use a black dermatograph pencil to draw the lines on the face very lightly. These are then covered with yellow greasepaint, using a thin brush (no. 6-8).

3 Use a fine brush to draw in extra yellow lines. The lips are also painted yellow.

4 Use white greasepaint to put highlights between the yellow lines on the cheeks and eyebrows..

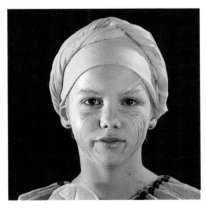

Useful hints
Doing the make-up for childres's parties requires a great deal of imagination. It is often better to suggest certain details (or use stylized effects) than to stick as closely as possible to nature in your make-up.

Lemon pattern

front and back

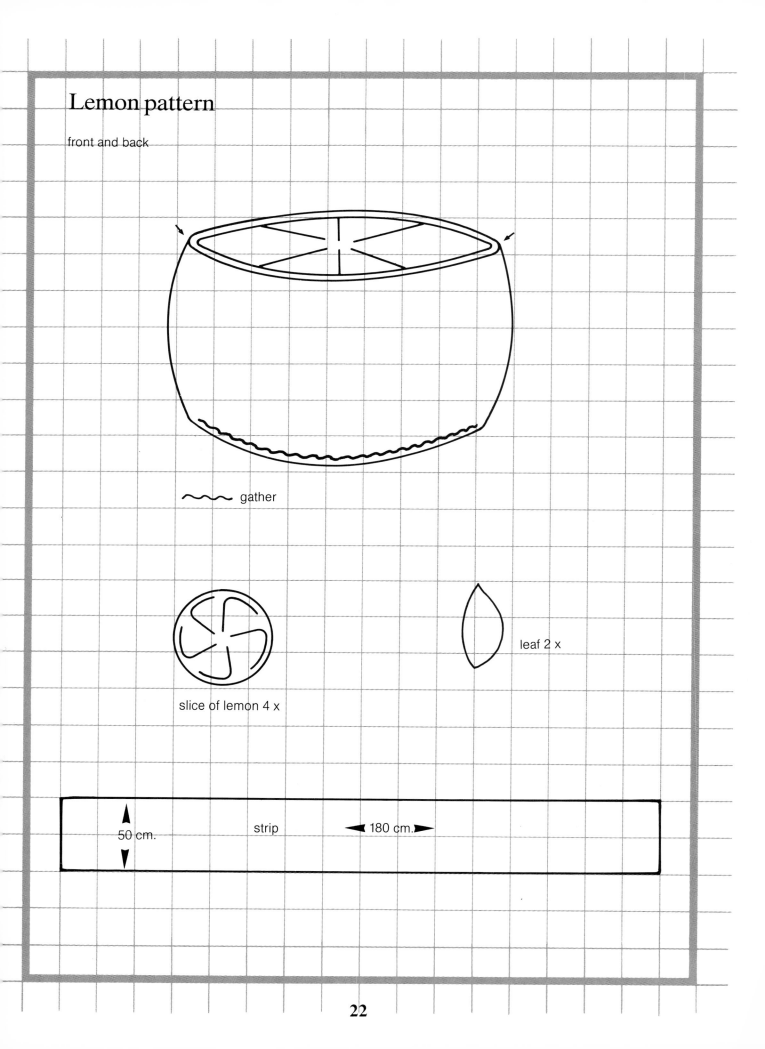

~~~ gather

slice of lemon 4 x

leaf 2 x

50 cm.

strip   ◄ 180 cm. ►

22

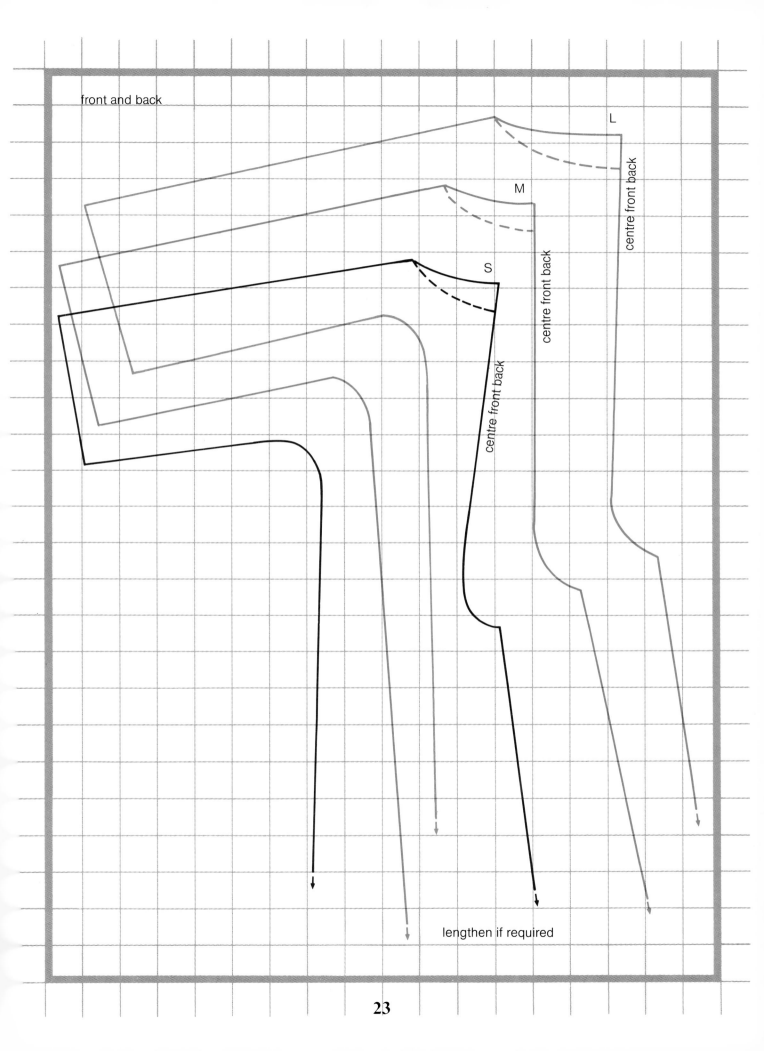

front and back

L

M

S

centre front back

centre front back

centre front back

centre front back

lengthen if required

23

Paprika

Material for the shirt
Pale yellow cotton or jersey 50 x 120 cm.

Material for cap and cloak
Red cotton jersey or similar material 120 x 120 cm.

In addition
Foam plastic 150 x 120 cm.
Remnant of green material
Hooks and eyes
Red braid or tape

◄1►
Cut shirt from pale yellow material.
◄2►
Stitch shoulder and side seams and part of the centre back seam.
◄3►
Finish of the neck edge with a hem, as well as the sleeves and bottom. Fasten with hooks and eyes.
◄4►
If required, gather sleeves with elastic.
◄5►
Cut the front and back of the paprika from the foam plastic.
◄6►
Place the foam plastic pieces on the red material and cut out, leaving a wide border.
◄7►
Stretch the material smooth, and pin.
◄8►
Use a small zig-zag stitch to stitch the material onto the foam plastic at the front. The foam plastic edge can easily be felt and pressed down while you are sewing.
◄9►
Cut away excess material.

◄10►
Follow the same steps for the cap (red material, foam plastic).
◄11►
Stitch the side seam of the cap and attach braid or tape.
◄12►
Cut the collar 4 x from plastic and red or green material. Stitch these in the same way as the rest. Stitch the side seams, fasten the collar with hooks and eyes.
◄13►
Stitch a number of leaves using foam plastic and green material, and attach to the costume.
◄14►
One collar piece used in the same way as above can serve as a foot cover (2 x). Stitch some red braid or tape to the sides and tie above the shoes.
◄15►
Fasten the bodice as folows:
a. Stitch the side seams and one shoulder seam. The other shoulder seam fastens with hooks and eyes.
b. Sew velcro onto all shoulder and side seams.

Accessories
Red or green tights.

Paprika

 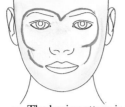 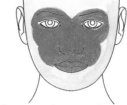 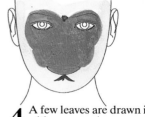

1 Use a sponge to apply pale pink and light yellow water-based paint.

2 The basic pattern is dwawn with red make-up.

3 The spaces between the lines are filled in with red make-up.

4 A few leaves are drawn in with green make-up.

Useful hints
For this make-up it is important to draw the lines very accurately so that the suggestion of the paprika is effective.

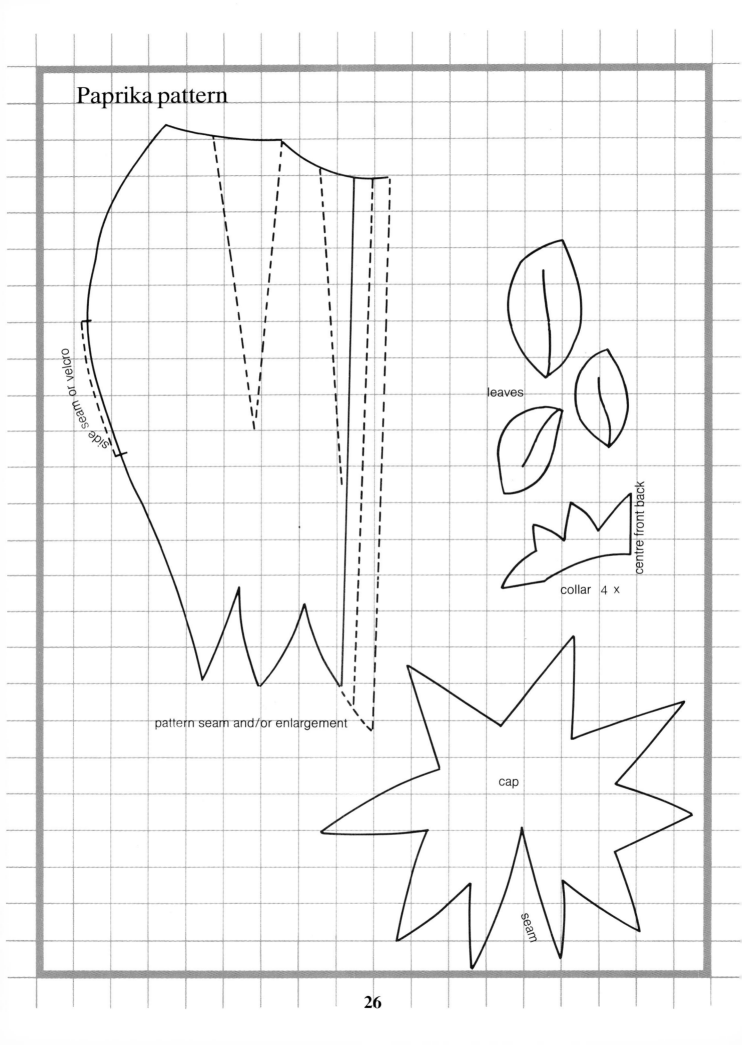

Paprika pattern

side seam or velcro

leaves

centre front back

collar 4 x

pattern seam and/or enlargement

cap

seam

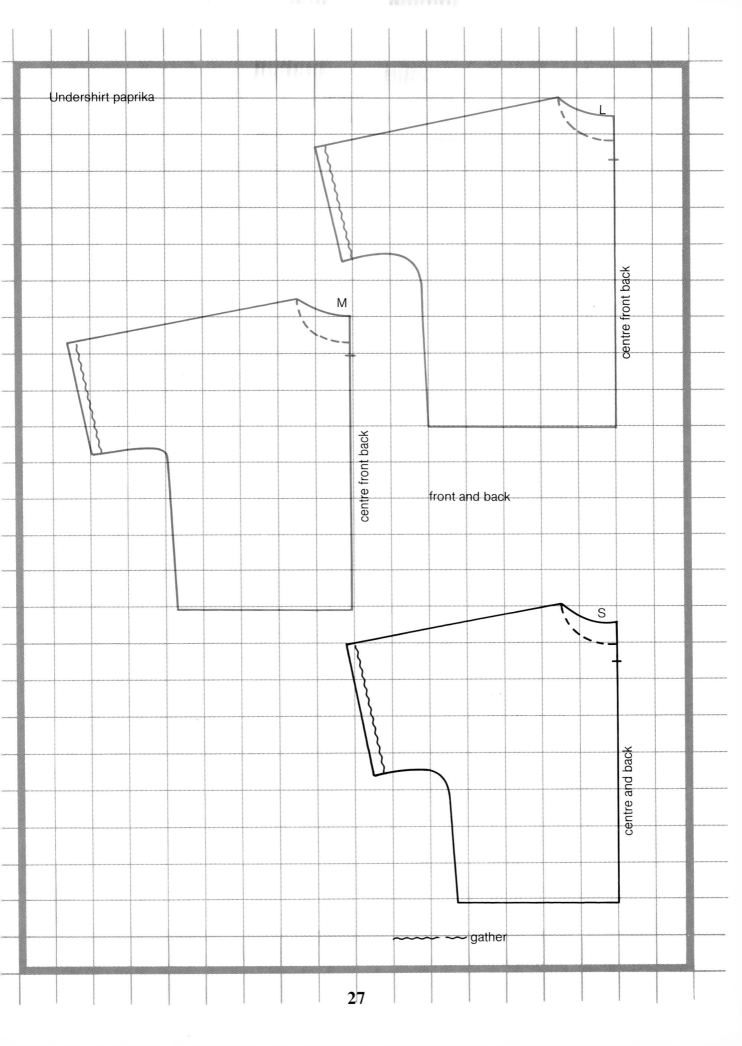

Undershirt paprika

L

centre front back

M

centre front back

front and back

S

centre and back

~~~ ~~ gather

27

Apple

Material for the jump suit and top
Green cotton jersey 220 x 100 cm
orange lining material 40 x 40 cm
Foam plastic 100 x 100 cm

Material for the shirt
White cotton 40 x 100 cm
Remnant of brown material for leaf, cap and stalk.

◀1▶
Cut leaves 2 x from the foam plastic.
◀2▶
Place foam plastic leaves on the green material and cut out 4 x leaving a wide margin.
◀3▶
Place the foam plastic leaves between two layers of material and smooth out the material. Pin material onto the foam plastic.
◀4▶
Stitch the side seams and inside leg seams together and turn trousers.
◀5▶
Stitch the material onto the foam plastic with a small zig-zag stitch along the edge. It is easy to feel the edge and press it flat while you are sewing.
◀6▶
Cut away excess material.
◀7▶
Cut the jump suit from the green material.
◀8▶
Stitch part of the centre back seam and the whole centre front seam.
◀9▶
Place the two pieces right sides together.
◀10▶
On the outside of the trouser legs fit in the leaves between the two layers. Pin the seams.
◀11▶
Stitch the side seams, shoulder seam and inside leg seam.
◀12▶
The leaves are stitched in and are visible when the jump suit is turned inside out. Finish the sleeves, trouser legs and neck with a small hem. Fasten the opening centre back with hooks and eyes.
◀13▶
If necessary, pass elastic through the neck, sleeves and trouser legs.
◀14▶
Cut the apple 2 x from the foam plastc.
◀15▶
Place the foam plastic shapes on the green material and cut out, leaving a generous border.

In addition
Velcro, hooks and eyes
Green and black felt tip for use on fabrics.

◀16
Stitch using a zig-zag stitch in the same way as the leaves.
◀17▶
Stitch the outlines of the 'bite' in the centre of the front with a zig-zag stitch. Then cut out the middle.
◀18▶
Cut an arbitrary piece from the orange material and stitch onto the front with a zig-zag stitch.
◀19▶
Stitch the shoulder seams.
◀20▶
Attach velcro to the sides of each piece.
◀21▶
Try the top on for size, and stitch the lines to make the pattern in the middle.
◀22▶
Cut the shirt from the cotton.
◀23▶
On the front of the shirt draw the apple core, so that it falls in the hole (the bite) of the top.
◀24▶
Stitch the shoulder seams and side seams. Stitch part of the centre back seam.
◀25▶
Finish off the arm holes, neck and bottom with a small hem. Fasten the opening with hooks and eyes.
◀26▶
Cut out the cap 3 x from the brown material. Stitch the pieces together. Hem round the bottom and pass elastic through to the required size.
◀27▶
Roll a cylinder from a remnant of foam plastic and cover this with brown material. Attach the stalk to the cap.
◀28▶
Make a leaf in the usual way with the foam plastic and brown material, and attach to the stalk.

Acessories
Dark brown boots or plimsolls.

Apple

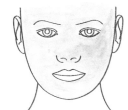 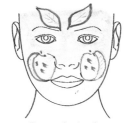  

1 Apply light brown water-based make-up with a sponge.

2 Draw the basic pattern with dark green make-up.

3 Fill in the open spaces with red and green water-based make-up.

4 The veins of the leaves are marked in with a thin brush, and the eyes are outlined in green.

Useful hints
The make-up described here serves as a starting point, but you can achieve your own personal creation using the techniques outlined above, and your own imagination. Your individual variations on the ideas given here, and personal experience are far more important than the slavish imitation of an example.

Apple pattern

front and back

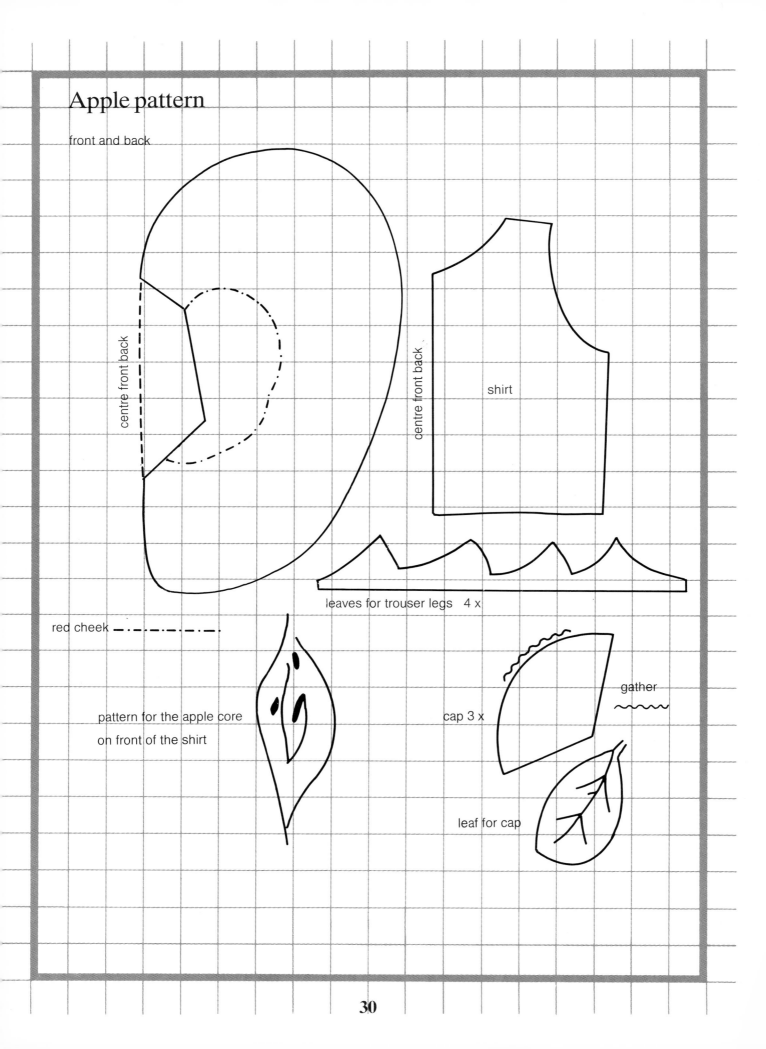

centre front back

centre front back

shirt

red cheek —·—·—·—·—

leaves for trouser legs 4 x

pattern for the apple core
on front of the shirt

cap 3 x

gather

leaf for cap

30

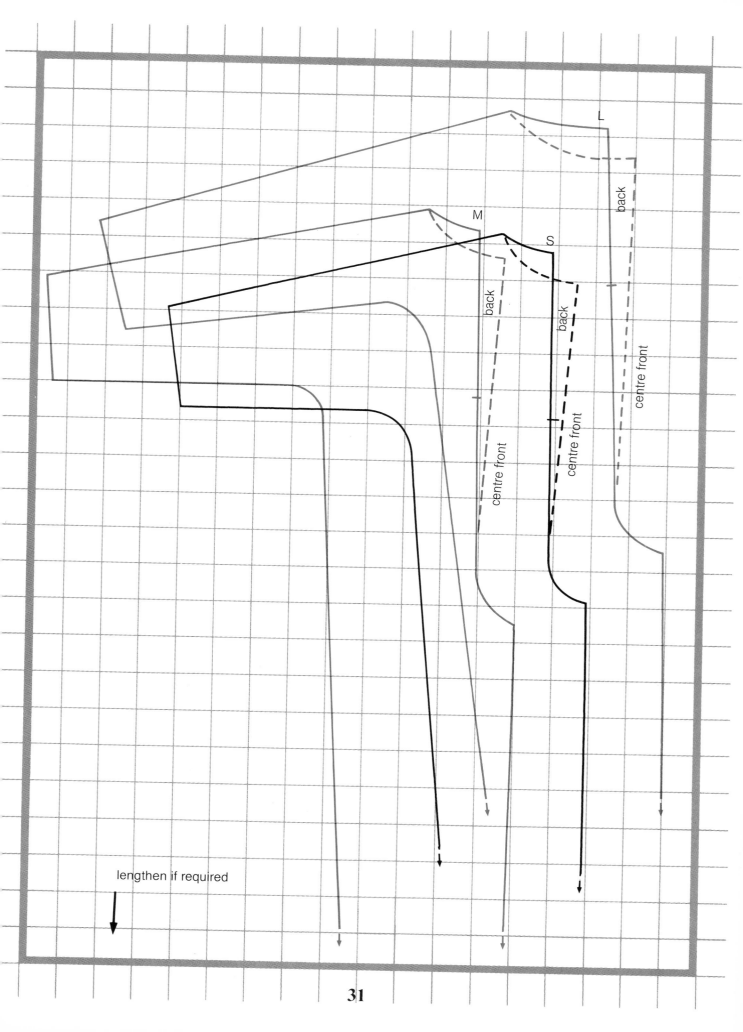

L

M

S

back

back

back

centre front

centre front

centre front

lengthen if required

31

Strawberry
Material for top
A red printed material 100 x 120 cm.

Material for collar and crown
Remnant of green material.

Material for cap
A remnant of red and/or printed material.

Material for shirt
Bright green jersey or cotton 80 x 120 cm.

In addition
hooks and eyes
elastic
foam plastic 120 x 120 cm.

◄1►
Cut the shirt from the green material.
◄2►
Stitch side, shoulder and centre back seam, leaving an opening at the end of the latter.
◄3►
Finish off neck, sleeves and bottom with a small hem.
◄4►
Pass elastic through the sleeves.
◄5►
Cut the strawberry pattern 2 x from the foam plastic.
◄6►
Place the foam plastic on the red material and cut out the shapes 2 x.
◄7►
Stretch the material over the foam plastic and pin. Stitch the material right side up onto the edge of the foam plastic with a small zig-zag stitch. It is easy to feel the edge and press it flat while you are sewing.
◄8►
Cut away the excess material.

◄9►
Stitch up side seams and one shoulder seam. The other shoulder seam can be fastened with hooks and eyes.
◄10►
Try on the top and stitch in darts for a good fit.
◄11►
Cut the collar from foam plastic and cover with red or green material. Fasten with hooks and eyes.
◄12►
Cut as many parts as you need for the cap from the foam plastic and the red material and sew in the same way as the top. Stitch the side seams of the cap.
◄13►
Use the pattern for the collar for the crown around the cap. Determine the right length yourself. Make the crown using green material and foam plastic.
◄14►
Make foot covers and attach round the foot with tape.

Accessoiries
Yellow tights

Strawberry

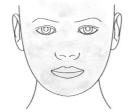   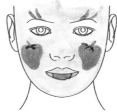

1 Lightish pink and yellow water-based make-up is applied thinly and evenly with a sponge. The colours merge slightly.

2 Draw the basic pattern with red make-up.

3 Colour in the lips with green make-up, reducing the size of the lower lip. Outline the eyelids with a dark colour and draw in the eyebrows.

4 Colour in the lips with green make-up, reducing the size of the lower lip. Outline the eyelids with a dark colour and draw in the eyebrows.

Useful hints
Start with a simple idea and gradually build up the make-up. It takes a great deal of practice to become proficient in the art of make-up.

Strawberry pattern

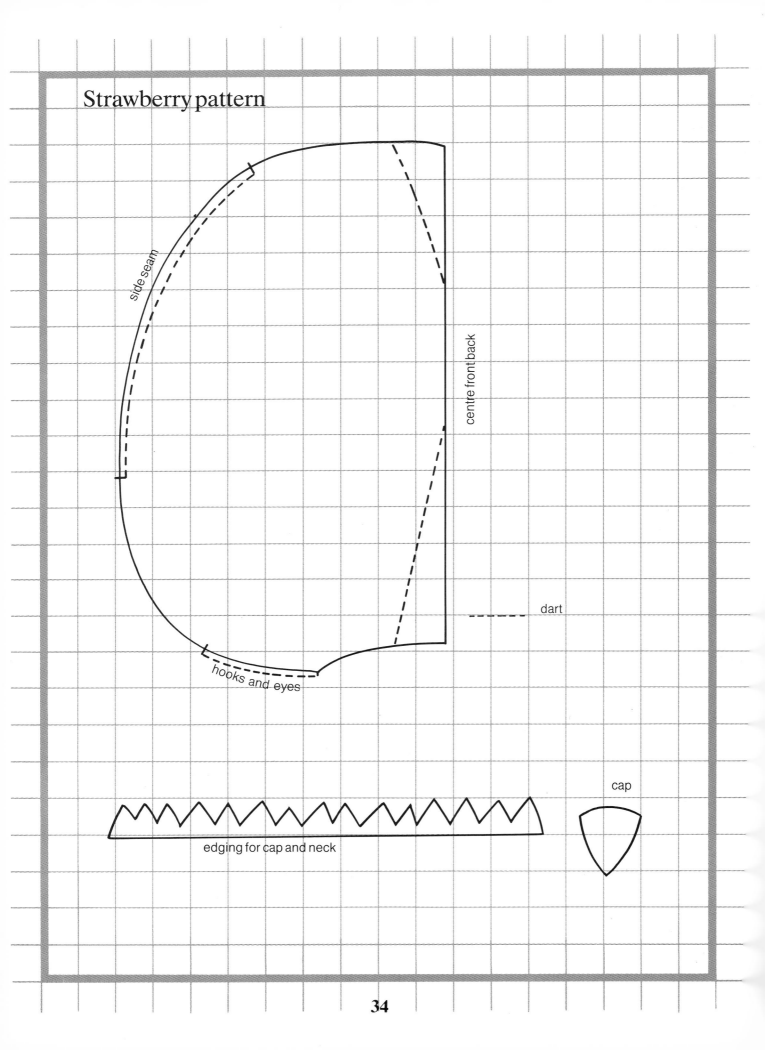

side seam

centre front back

dart

hooks and eyes

edging for cap and neck

cap

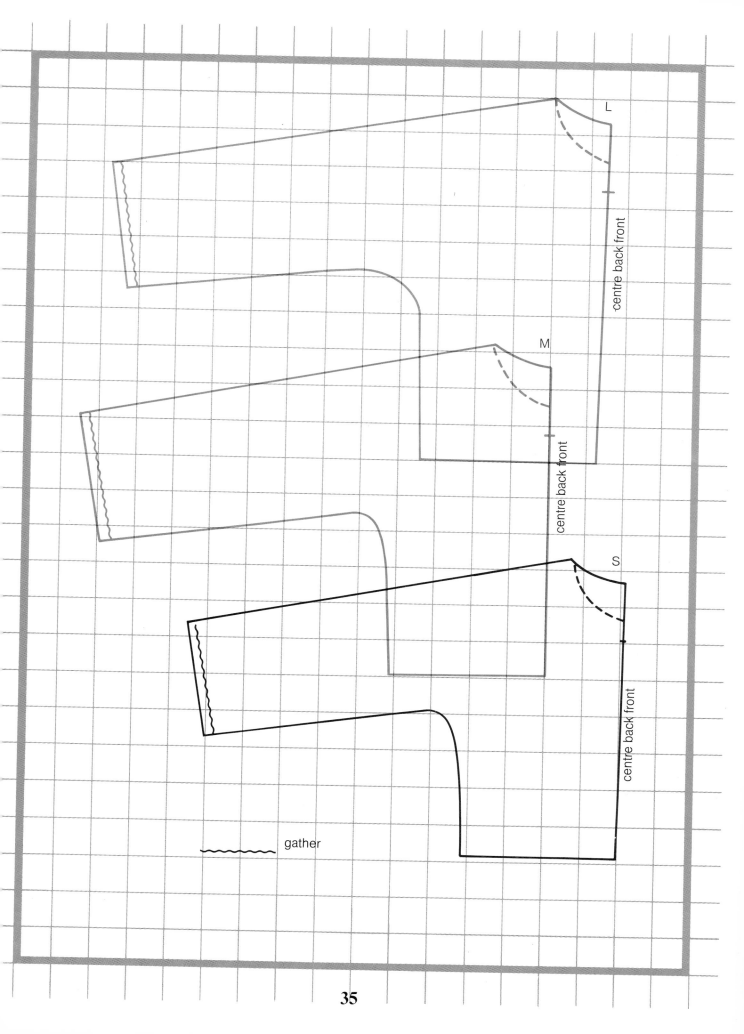

centre back front

L

M

centre back front

centre back front

S

centre back front

～～～～ gather

35

Grape

Material for shirt
Pale yellow or mauve cotton 50 x 120 cm.

Material for trousers
Mauve jersey or cotton 70 x 120 cm.

Material for top
Purplish blue jersey 50 x 120 cm.
Foam plastic 50 x 120 cm.

◄1►
Cut out shirt.
◄2►
Stitch shoulder and side seams. Stitch part of centre back seam.
◄3►
Fasten opening with hooks and eyes.
◄4►
Finish off sleeves, neck and bottom with a small hem.
◄5►
Cut the pattern for the bunch of grapes 1 x from the foam plastic.
◄6►
Place the foam plastic pattern on the purplish blue material nd cut out leaving a generous border.
◄7►
Stretch the material on the foam plastic and pin.
◄8►
Stitch the material onto the edge of the foam plastic on the front with a small zig-zag stitch. You can easily feel the edge of the foam plastic and press it flat when you are stitching.
◄9►
Cut away excess material and stitch lines to pattern.
◄10►
Make the leaves in the same way, using white material and foam plastic (about 8 x).
◄11►
Cut two wide bands from the remaining purplish blue material and hem these. Attach these tapes to the back of the grape at waist height and tie up the back.
◄12►
Cut a headband from the remaining white or purplish blue material. Hem the headband and dye if necessary.

Material for leaves
White cotton jersey 30 x 120 cm.
Foam plastic 30 x 120 cm.

In addition
One tin of red, green and yellow fabric dye, elastic, hooks and eyes

◄13►
Prepare the yellow dye using, half a tin. Dye the leaves according to the instructions, rinse thoroughly, but do not allow to dry.
◄14►
Prepare the green dye, using half a tin. Submerge some of the leaves in this about halfway, moving constantly while the dye is being absorbed. Rinse thoroughly and leave to dry. Then iron with a cool iron.
◄15►
Prepare the red dye, using half a tin. Submerge the remaining leaves halfway, moving constantly while the dye is being absorbed. Rinse thoroughly and leave to dry. Then iron with a cool iron.
◄16►
Attach vine leaves to headband and a bunch of grapes.
◄17►
Cut the trousers from mauve material. Stitch the side, front and back seams. Finish off the top and trouser legs with a small hem, and pass elastic through these. If the material is fairly heavy, the top can be reinforced with an extra band.

N.B. It is also possible to hang the bunch of grapes round the neck by a thin tape to which some leaves can also be attached.

Accessories
A thin pair of tights.
Shoes on which a few leaves can be tied.

For boys
Boys could wear a jump suit instead of the harem trousers and shirt.

Grape

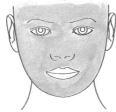 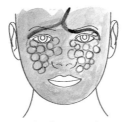 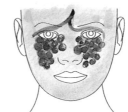 

1 A light bright purple water-based make-up is applied to the face thinly and evenly.

2 The lines are drawn on the face with a black dermatograph pencil. The stalk of the bunch of grapes is drawn with a brown pencil.

3 The grapes are filled in with dark purple water-based make-up.

4 The lips are painted a wine red colour, and the lines around the eyes are emphasized.

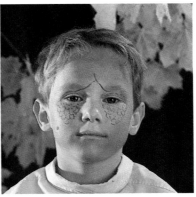

Useful hints
Always use a light foundation so that the colour emerges more clearly.

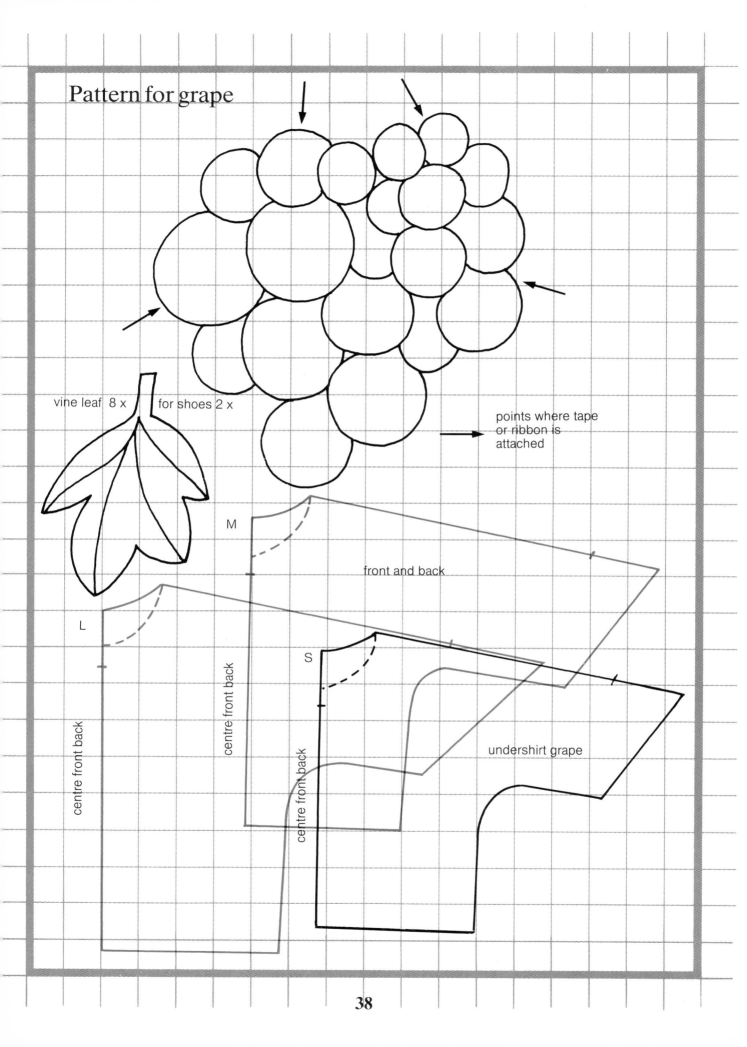

Pattern for grape

vine leaf 8 x   for shoes 2 x

points where tape
or ribbon is
attached

M

front and back

L

centre front back

centre front back

S

centre front back

undershirt grape

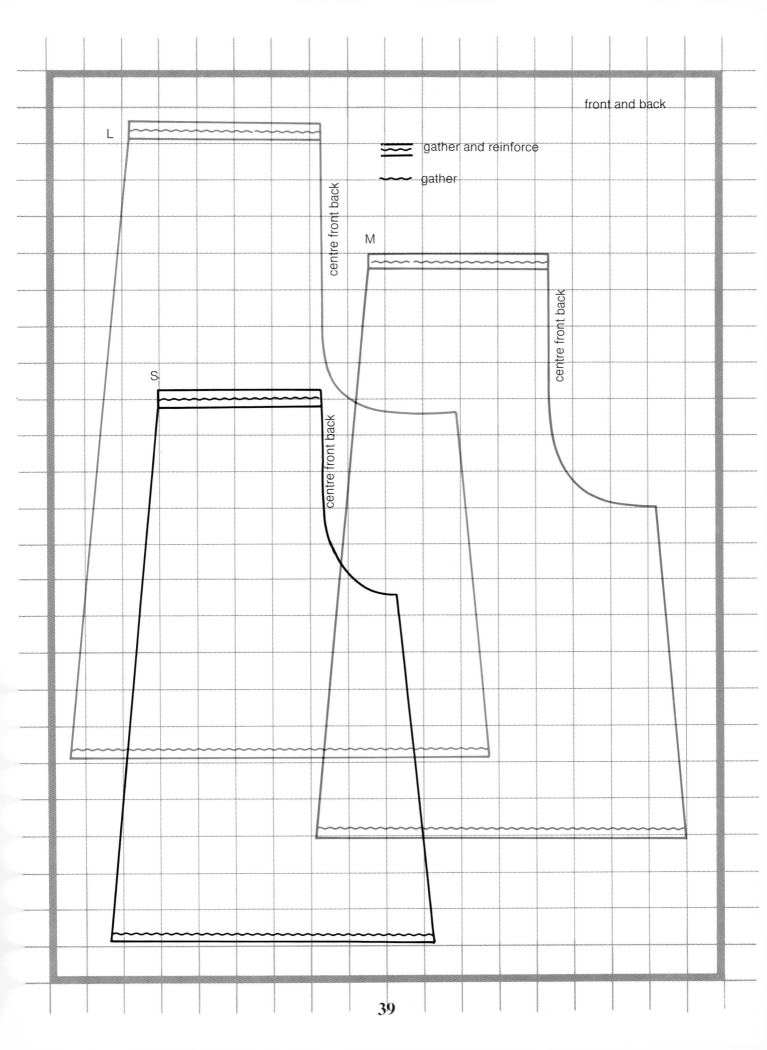

front and back

gather and reinforce

gather

L

centre front back

M

centre front back

S

centre front back

39

Pear
Material for the jump suit
Brown jersey 120 x 120 cm.

Material for pear
White cotton jersey (washed), 100 x 120 cm.
Foam plastic 100 x 150 cm.

In addition
One green or yellow elasticated hairband
Elastic, hooks and eyes, velcro
One tin of yellow fabric dye
One tin of green fabric dye
One tin of orange fabric dye

◄1►
Cut out the jump suit.
◄2►
Stitch up seams.
◄3►
Finish neck, sleeves and trouser legs with a small hem.
◄4►
If necessary, pass elastic through the hem at the neck.
◄5►
Fasten the centre back with hooks and eyes.
◄6►
Cut the larger pear from the foam plastic (2x).
◄7►
Cut this shape from the white jersey (2 x), leaving a very generous border.
◄8►
Stretch the jersey over the foam plastic and pin the material.
◄9►
Stitch the material right side up, exactly onto the edge of the foam plastic with a small zig-zag stitch. It is easy to feel the edge and press down while you are stitching. Cut away excess material along the zig-zag edge.
◄10►
The same steps are followed for the small pear (3 x) and leaf (5 x).
◄11►
The seams forming the pattern for veins in the leaves etc. are stitched into all the pieces of foam plastic.

◄12►
Prepare the yellow dye. Dye the large pear, small pear and leaves according to the instructions, rinse thoroughly. Do not allow to dry.
◄13►
Prepare the orange dye. Submerge the bottom or top part of the pear in the dye, moving constantly so that there will be no sharp line separating the colours. Rinse thoroughly but do not allow to dry.
◄14►
Prepare the green dye. Submerge the top or bottom part of the pears and the leaves in the dye and follow the instructions in no. 13.
◄15►
Spin dry all the pieces and dry. Iron with a cool iron.
◄16►
Make a stalk for the large pear (2 x) using a remnant of foam plastic, and stitch a strip of velcro onto the inside. Sew the stalks onto the pear.
◄17►
Attach the sides with velcro or tape. Try the costume on first.
◄18►
Attach a few small pears and leaves onto the hairband.

Accessories
Plimsolls and possibly tights in a matching colour. Small pears or leaves can be attached to the plimsolls.

Pear

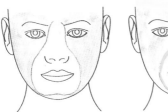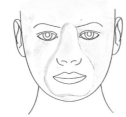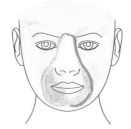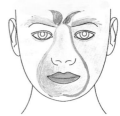

1 The basic pattern is drawn on the face with green water-based make-up, using a thin brush. The greenish colour is applied with water-based make-up.

2 A pale yellow water-based make-up is applied evenly to the forehead. A yellow outline is drawn with a brush.

3 An orange outline is drawn with a brush. The colour merges into a red shade which is applied on the cheek and chin.

4 The lips are painted red and the eyebrows are emphasized with brown make-up.

Useful hints
Try to maintain a balance between the right and left halves of the face.

Pear pattern

front and back
(mirror image)

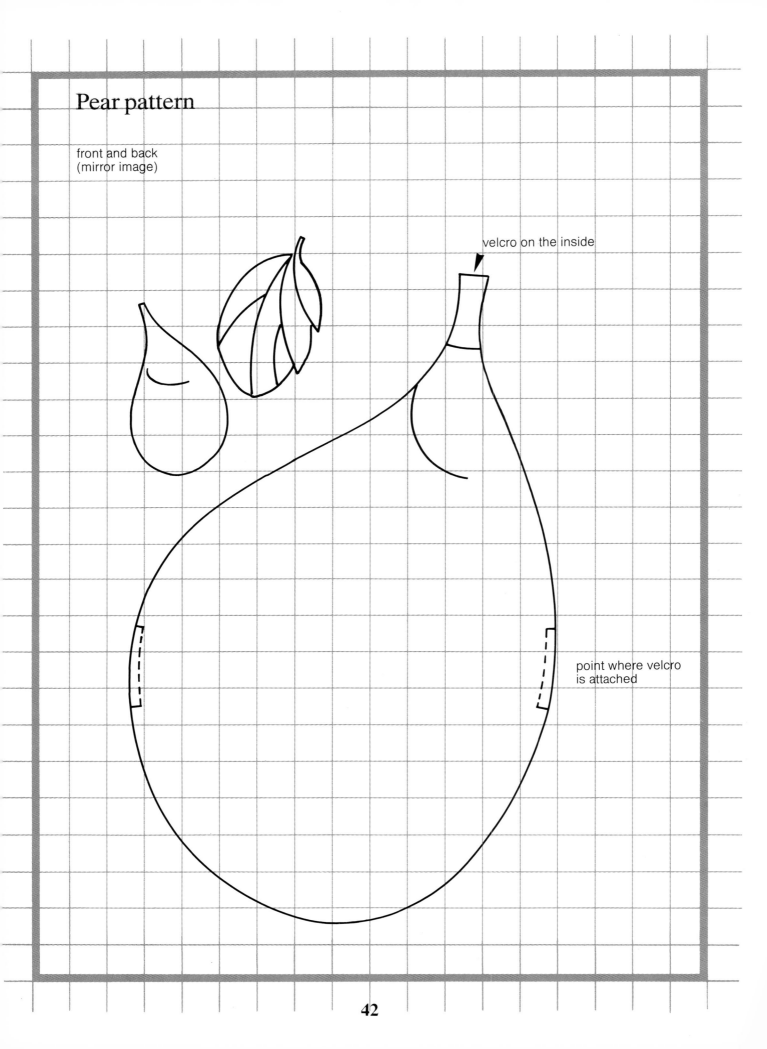

velcro on the inside

point where velcro
is attached

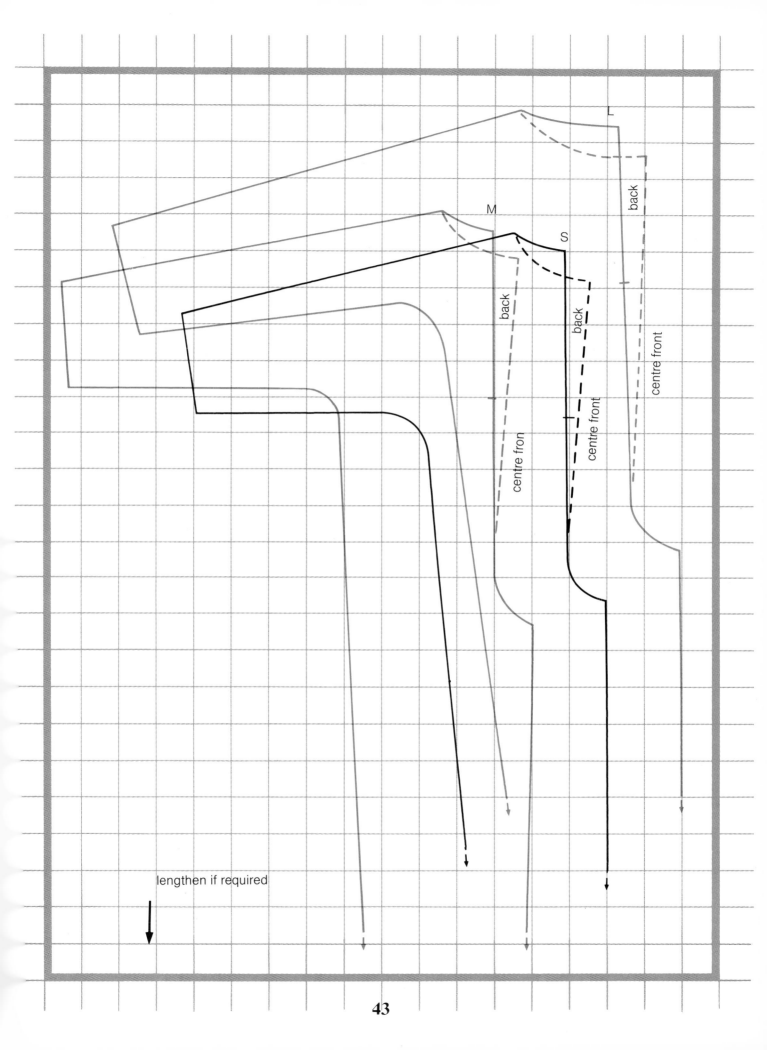

M

L

S

back

back

back

centre fron

centre front

centre front

lengthen if required

Cucumber

Material for dress and hat
White cotton (washed) 220 x 120 cm.
Foam plastic 60 x 120 cm.

In addition
a fine yellow or green shawl
elastic
a tin of yellow, green, blue and orange fabric dye

◄1►
Cut the dress from the white material. Cut the required length for the cucumber straight at the bottom.
◄2►
Stitch side and shoulder seams.
◄3►
Finish off sleeves and neck edge with a small hem and pass elastic through this. (This can also be done after the material has been dyed.)
◄4►
Stitch a border of foam plastic the same width as the cucumber edge on the inside of the dress.
◄5►
Draw the cucumbers on the right side of the material.
◄6►
Stitch the pattern with a small zig-zag stitch.
◄7►
Cut away excess material along the zig-zag edge.
◄8►
Cut the parts for the hat and the other cucumbers from foam plastic. If cucumbers are also used on the shoes, cut out 4 x.
◄9►
Place the pieces for the hat and the cucumbers on the white material and cut out leaving a generous border.
◄10►
Smooth the material on these pieces and pin. Stitch the material onto the foam plastic right side up with a small zig-zag stitch. It is easy to feel the edge of the foam plastic and press it down when you are stitching.
◄11►
Cut away excess material along the zig-zag edge.
◄12►
Prepare the green dye.
◄13►
Follow the instructions to dye all the cucumbers and pieces for the hat. Rinse thoroughly, spin dry and hang out to dry. Then iron with a cool iron.
◄14►
Use the same solution to dye the bottom half of the dress, moving it constantly in the dye so that there is not a sharply defined border of colour. Rinse thoroughly but do not allow to dry.

◄15►
Prepare the blue dye and dye the top of the dress in the same way. Rinse thoroughly and dry.
◄16►
Cut out long strips of material for the edge of the skirt and the collar. Join the strips together. Finish off the edges of the collar with a hem. Hem the strip for the skirt on one side.
◄17►
Prepare the orange dye.
◄18►
Fold the strips for the skirt and neck over a few times and submerge partly in the dye. Follow the instructions, rinse but do not allow to dry.
◄19►
Prepare the yellow dye.
◄20►
Submerge the other half of the material in the yellow dye. When the dye has been absorbed, rinse thoroughly, dry, and iron the material.
◄21►
Gather the strip for the skirt and stitch under the cucumber edge.
◄22►
Pass elastic through the strip for the neck and fasten with hooks and eyes.
◄23►
Stitch the parts of the hat together. If it is too wide, it can be made to fit by stitching darts in the centre of the panels.
◄24►
Sew the shawl onto the point of the hat.
◄25►
Sew the cucumbers onto the dress and, if required, onto the shoes.

Accessories
matching tights
shoes

For boys
Use a pattern for one of the jump suits. Sew the same cucumber edge onto the edge of the sleeves and trouser legs, as the edge used on the skirt. The other cucumbers are sewn on in the same way. A yellowy orange shawl is tied around the waist.

Cucumber

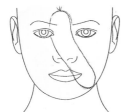 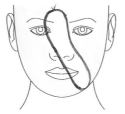 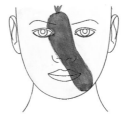 

1 A yellowish-brown water-based make-up is applied with a sponge.

2 Use dark green make-up to draw the basic pattern.

3 Fill up the open space with dark green water-based make-up. Draw a small crown at the top of the cucumber with brown make-up.

4 Fill up the open space with dark green water-based make-up.

Useful hints
The powder that is used should be very fine. The finer it is, the more transparent the effect that is produced. Coarse powder covers too much, so that little of the basic make-up shows through. The colour of the powder should always be lighter than the foundation, as the former will be too strong when it is mixed.

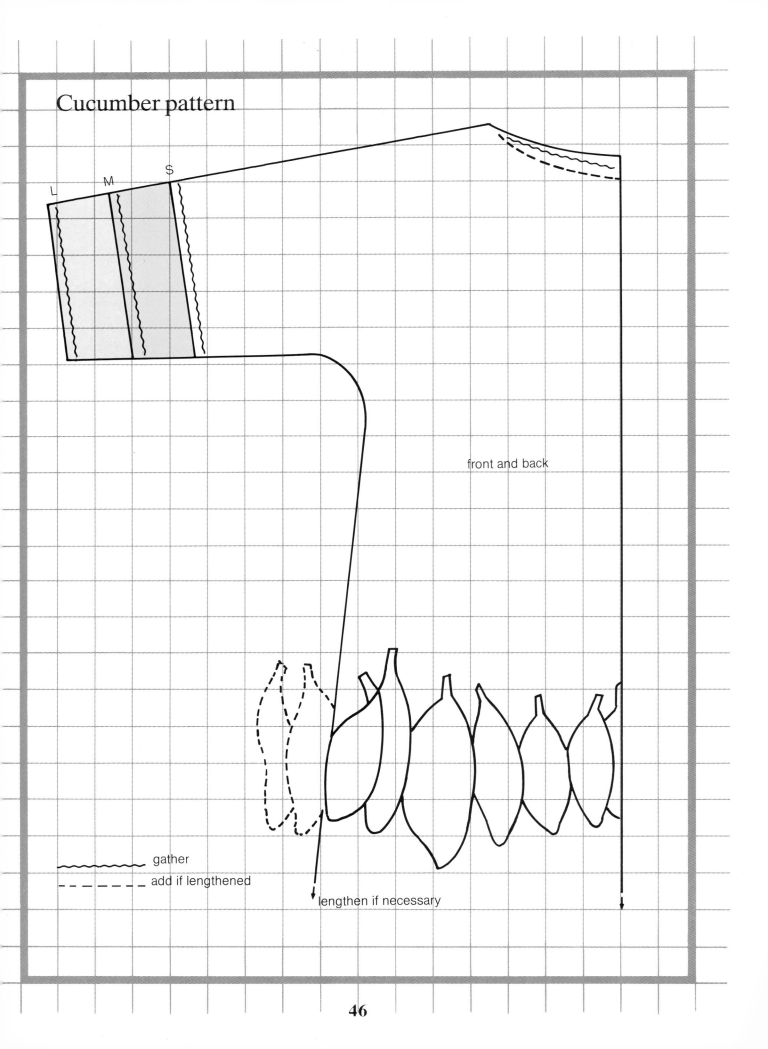

Cucumber pattern

L M S

front and back

gather

add if lengthened

lengthen if necessary

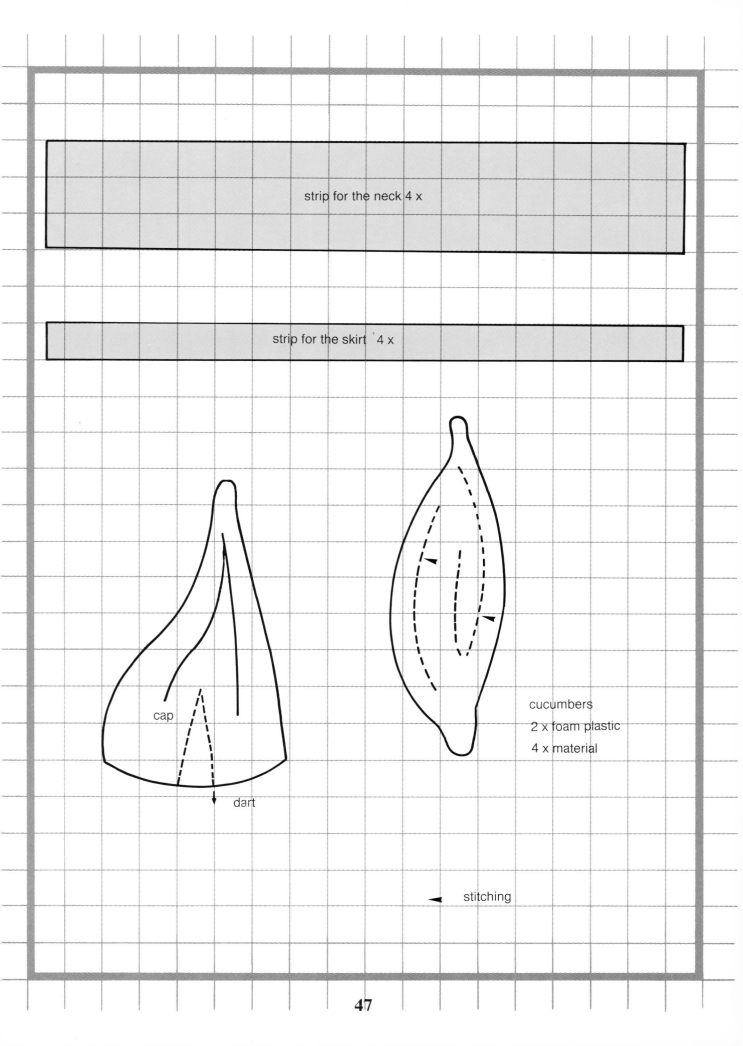

strip for the neck 4 x

strip for the skirt ' 4 x

cap

dart

cucumbers

2 x foam plastic

4 x material

stitching

Raspberry

Material for shirt
Bright green lining or cotton 50 x 120 cm.
Material for dress, hat, collar and armband
Red cotton jersey 140 x 120 cm.
Foam plastic 200 x 120 cm.

In addition
hooks and eyes
elastic

◄1►
Cut out shirt.
◄2►
Stitch up side seams, shoulder seam and part of centre back seam.
◄3►
Finish off sleeves, bottom and neck with a small hem. Pass elastic through the sleeves. Fasten opening with hooks and eyes.
◄4►
Cut the dress from the red material.
◄5►
Stitch side seams and shoulder seams. Finish off armholes and neck with a small hem.
◄6►
Stitch up part of the centre back seam. Fasten the opening with hooks and eyes.
◄7►
From the foam plastic, cut a strip 20 cm. wide and as long as the circumference of the bottom of the dress.
◄8►
Pin the foam plastic onto the inside of the dress.
◄9►
Draw the outlines of the raspberries on the outside of the dress.
◄10►
Stitch along these lines with a small zig-zag stitch and cut away excess material along the bottom.
◄11►
Cut the yoke from the foam plastic, place the foam plastic yoke on the red material and cut out, leaving a generous border.
◄12►
Smooth the material over the foam plastic and pin.
◄13►
Stitch the material along the edge of the foam plastic with a small zig-zag stitch and cut away the excess material. Stitch up seams. Stitch along the outlines of the raspberry.

◄1►
Fasten the collar with hooks and eyes.
◄14►
Cut the hat from foam plastic.
◄15►
Also cut the hat from the red material, leaving a generous border. Smooth the material over the pieces of the hat and stitch down with a large zig-zag stitch. Cut away the excess material.
◄16►
Stitch the seams of the hat, try it on, and if necessary, stitch darts in the centre of the panels.
◄17►
Stitch a wide hem along the bottom of the hat.
◄18►
Place the remaining red material on the remaining foam plastic and cut out approximately 60 circles with a diameter of 8 cm.
◄19►
Tack around the circles with strong thread. Gather the thread to make little balls.
◄20►
Sew the balls down onto the hat.
◄21►
Make an armband with the left over pieces of material and attach some balls to it.

Accessories
red tights
shoes

For boys
Make a sleeveless jump suit instead of a dress. The green shirt can also be worn with this. The collar and hat remain the same. This costume is finished off with a wide belt with raspberry balls, worn round the waist.

Raspberry

1 The face is made up thinly and evenly with a light pink make-up.

2 Apply some greenish water-based make-up evenly to some of the rest of the face.

3 The mouth is drawn in.

4 Fill in the mouth with red make-up. Use green make-up to draw the eyebrows and outline the eyes with a reddish-brown colour to emphasize them.

Useful hints
With greasepaint it is necessary to use powder. This serves to fix the make-up and prevent shiny patches on the face. A good light neutral powder is patted onto the make-up with a powder puff (never rub it in), and the excess powder is then brushed away with a powder brush.

Raspberry pattern

front and back

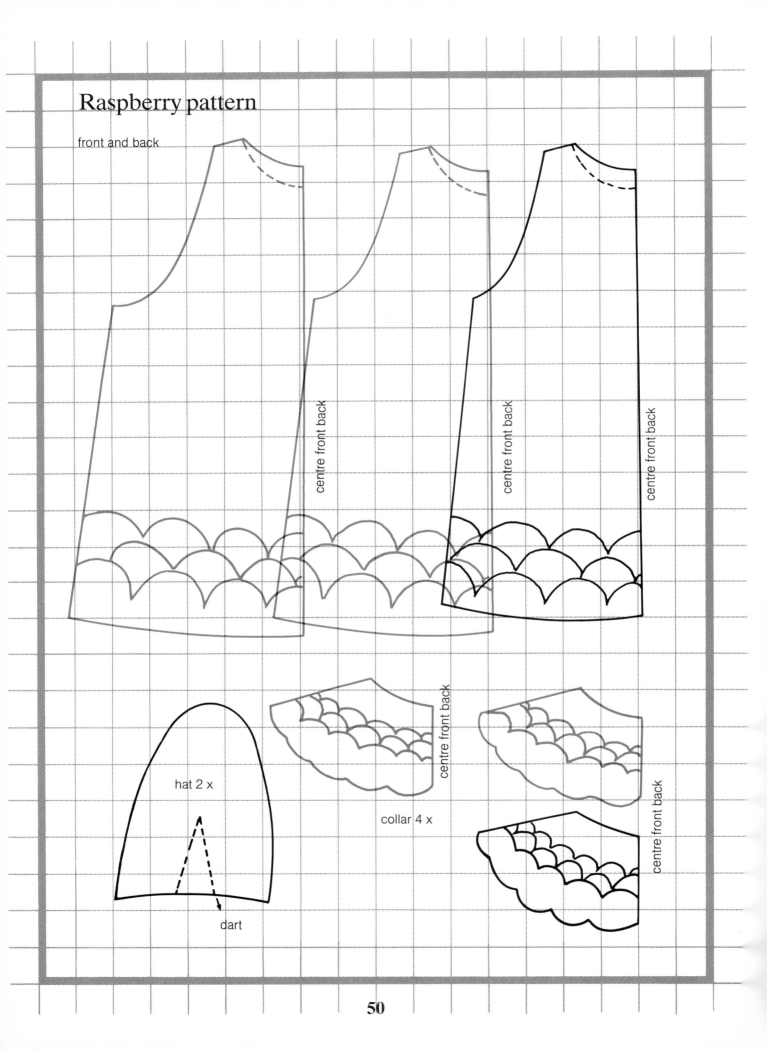

centre front back

centre front back

centre front back

hat 2 x

dart

collar 4 x

centre front back

centre front back

centre front back

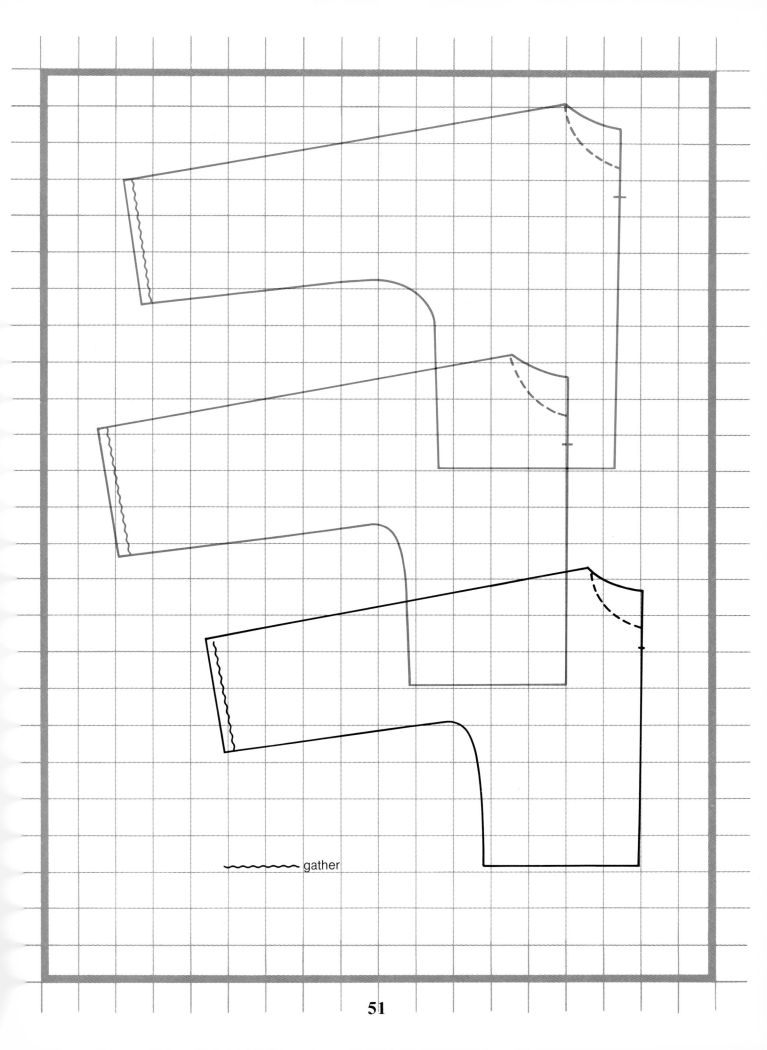

~~~~~~~ gather